Budget Without Worry:

Your Guide to Financial Calm

PUBLISHED BY: Joshua B Rhoades

Copyright © 2024 by Joshua B Rhoades
All rights reserved.
ISBN: 9798305638424

Table of Contents

Budget Without Worry: 1

Your Guide to Financial Calm 1

Introduction 5

Conclusion 8

Common Misconceptions About Budgeting 9

Conclusion 13

What You'll Gain from This Book 14

Chapter 1: Facing Your Financial Reality 16

Chapter 2: 25

Setting the Foundation with Goals 25

Chapter 3: Mastering the Basics of Budgeting 33

Quiz Questions to Refine Your Choice 41

Final Tips 42

Setting Up Your First Budget 43

Chapter 4: Tracking and Adjusting 46

Chapter 5: Overcoming Common Challenges 55

Dealing with Irregular Income 60

Managing Setbacks Without Guilt 66

Chapter 6: Building Savings and Security 70

Chapter 7: Creating Long-Term Financial Habits 84

Chapter 8: Thriving with Your New Budget 95

Conclusion 104

Your Financial Freedom Plan 105

Final Motivation 109

Financial Goal-Setting Worksheets 113

Recommended Budgeting Apps and Tools 114

Introduction

Why Budgeting Matters

The Importance of Financial Health and Its Impact on Overall Well-Being

Financial health is not just about having enough money—it's about how well you manage and make decisions with your finances. The state of your financial health directly affects your emotional, physical, and mental well-being, and it influences many aspects of your life, including relationships, career choices, and future opportunities.

Emotional and Mental Well-Being

When you do not have a solid financial plan, stress often takes over. Constant worrying about bills, debt, or whether you will make ends meet can lead to anxiety, depression, and even physical symptoms like insomnia, headaches, and fatigue. The pressure to manage unplanned expenses or living paycheck to paycheck can weigh heavily on your mind, reducing your capacity to focus on other important aspects of life.

Conversely, when you have a handle on your finances, you gain a sense of security and control. This reduces stress, promotes a sense of accomplishment, and boosts self-esteem.

Feeling financially stable means, you are better able to navigate challenges without feeling overwhelmed, and you're more capable of focusing on personal growth and long-term goals.

Physical Health

Financial struggles are linked to poor physical health. The stress of financial insecurity can contribute to unhealthy behaviors such as overeating, smoking, or avoiding medical care due to cost concerns. People under financial stress often experience higher levels of cortisol, the hormone associated with stress, which can lead to high blood pressure, heart disease, and weakened immune systems.

On the other hand, financial stability can lead to healthier lifestyle choices. With a stable income and a budget that includes funds for healthcare, exercise, and healthy food, you're more likely to prioritize well-being and invest in long-term health. This can lead to a better quality of life and improved longevity.

Relationships and Social Well-Being

Financial problems can cause strain on relationships, leading to arguments and even breakups in romantic partnerships or family disputes over money matters. The tension created by money struggles can prevent meaningful communication and affect how individuals connect with one another.

However, when you have clear financial goals and a solid plan in place, you create a sense of unity and shared purpose with your loved ones. Couples who manage finances together can experience increased trust and stability. Financial health allows families to spend quality time together without the constant stress of financial concerns.

Career and Opportunities

Financial stability opens more career opportunities and the ability to take calculated risks. If you're financially secure, you may feel more confident in exploring new job opportunities, starting a business, or pursuing further education. This freedom also enables you to focus on your career goals without the distraction of financial insecurity.

Additionally, being financially healthy allows you to plan for important life milestones—like buying a home, traveling, or even retiring—without the burden of excessive debt or living paycheck to paycheck.

Achieving Personal Goals

Financial health acts as the foundation upon which all of your goals can be built. Whether it's buying a home, traveling the world, pursuing hobbies, or saving for retirement, achieving personal dreams becomes far more achievable when your finances are in order. Having a clear financial picture not only allows you to pursue your desires but also gives you peace of mind knowing that you're actively working toward your future, instead of simply surviving from month to month.

Conclusion

The link between financial health and overall well-being is undeniable. By managing your finances effectively, you're not just ensuring that your needs are met—you're setting the stage for a happier, healthier, and more fulfilling life. Budgeting, saving, and planning for the future may feel like a daunting task at first, but it's an investment in your mental, physical, and emotional health. Financial health empowers you to live a life free of unnecessary stress, enabling you to focus on what truly matters—your happiness, relationships, and dreams.

Common Misconceptions About Budgeting

Many people resist budgeting because they believe it's a complex or overly restrictive process. These misconceptions can prevent individuals from experiencing the full benefits of financial control and freedom. In reality, budgeting is a flexible, empowering tool that helps you achieve your goals without feeling deprived. Let's address some of the most common myths about budgeting:

1. "Budgeting is Too Complicated."

One of the biggest barriers people face when it comes to budgeting is the belief that it's too complicated. Many envision spreadsheets filled with complex formulas or think they need to track every cent down to the penny.

Reality: Budgeting doesn't have to be complicated. In fact, the simpler the system, the more likely you are to stick with it. Tools like budgeting apps (e.g., YNAB, Mint, or even simple Excel spreadsheets) simplify the process by automatically categorizing your expenses, offering clear insights into where your money is going. You don't need to track every tiny expense—

just focus on the big categories like housing, transportation, groceries, and entertainment.

Once you develop the habit of budgeting, it becomes second nature. You can start with a basic system and adjust as you go. Remember, budgeting is about making informed choices, not overcomplicating the process.

2. "Budgets Are Too Restrictive."

Another common misconception is that budgeting means you must cut out everything fun or spontaneous. People often think that once they set a budget, they won't have the freedom to enjoy themselves.

Reality: A budget is not about depriving yourself—it's about making intentional decisions with your money. You can absolutely have fun within a budget! By prioritizing your needs and wants, you can allocate money for things that bring you joy—whether it's dining out, traveling, or enjoying hobbies. A budget ensures you can afford those things without feeling guilty or stressed, and helps you avoid overspending or falling into debt.

When you set financial goals, such as saving for a vacation or buying something important, your budget will help you get there while still allowing for enjoyment along the way. The key is finding balance, not restricting your life.

3. "Budgets Are Only for People Who Are Struggling with Money."

Some people believe that budgeting is only necessary for those facing financial difficulties, or that it's a sign of being "bad with money." As a result, they may feel that they don't need to budget if they're already financially stable.

Reality: Everyone can benefit from budgeting, regardless of their financial situation. Even if you're doing well financially, a budget is still a powerful tool that helps you maximize your savings, invest for the future, and reach your goals. For instance, budgeting can help you plan for retirement, pay off debt faster, or save for big life events like buying a house or funding your children's education. It ensures that you're not leaving money on the table and helps you make smarter, more intentional financial choices.

The more you plan, the more you can achieve—and budgeting helps make that planning easier.

4. "Budgeting Means Sacrificing Everything I Want."

Another misconception is that budgeting will force you to give up all the things you love—like coffee, dining out, or weekend trips.

Reality: Budgeting is about prioritization, not elimination. The goal is to create a spending plan that allows you to enjoy your life while still being responsible with your finances. If dining out is important to you, for example, you can allocate a certain amount each month for it. The key is not to go overboard and end up in debt, but to make sure that what you value is still accounted for in your budget.

Budgeting allows you to strike a balance between enjoying life today and planning for your future. Rather than focusing on what you "can't" have, budgeting helps you identify what's most important and ensure that you can afford it without guilt.

5. "I Have to Be Perfect with My Budget or It's Pointless."

Some people think that budgeting requires perfection—every expense must be accounted for, and any mistakes will derail their entire plan.

Reality: Budgeting is a dynamic process. Life is unpredictable, and things don't always go as planned. A small misstep or deviation from your budget doesn't mean failure. In fact, part of budgeting is learning how to adjust as circumstances change. If you go over budget in one category, you can shift funds from another category to make up for it, or re-evaluate and make changes for the next month.

The goal of budgeting is to stay in control of your finances and move towards your goals, not to be perfect. The more you practice, the more comfortable you'll become with adjusting your plan when necessary.

6. "I Don't Make Enough Money to Budget."

People often think that only those with larger incomes need to budget—if you don't earn much, budgeting seems unnecessary or unattainable.

Reality: Budgeting is essential for everyone, regardless of income level. In fact, budgeting becomes even more important when you have a limited income because it allows you to make the most of what you have. It helps you prioritize spending, save for emergencies, and plan for the future, even on a smaller income. Small, consistent savings and mindful spending can build up over time, leading to financial stability and freedom. You may be surprised by how much you can achieve with even a modest income if you budget effectively.

7. "Budgeting Takes Too Much Time."

Some believe that budgeting requires a lot of time and effort, which can deter them from starting. They fear it will take hours to organize finances and track every detail.

Reality: Budgeting doesn't need to consume all your time. In fact, once you set up your budget, it only takes a few minutes each week or month to review and adjust. There are numerous apps and tools that automate the process, track your expenses, and even help you stay on target. Budgeting becomes easier with practice, and the time you invest initially will pay off in terms of less stress and better financial control.

Conclusion

These misconceptions often prevent people from embracing budgeting and experiencing the benefits it offers. The truth is, budgeting is a flexible, empowering tool that helps you take control of your finances and achieve your dreams. It's not about restriction, complexity, or perfection—it's about making conscious, informed decisions with your money to build the life you want. With the right mindset and approach, budgeting can open doors to financial freedom, security, and peace of mind.

What You'll Gain from This Book

Budgeting is a fundamental practice that offers numerous benefits, significantly enhancing your financial well-being and overall quality of life. Here are some key advantages:

1. Reduces Financial Stress

By providing a clear overview of your income and expenses, budgeting helps you live within your means, reducing the anxiety associated with financial uncertainty. It enables you to anticipate and prepare for upcoming expenses, leading to a more relaxed and secure financial state.

2. Helps Achieve Financial Goals

Budgeting allows you to set and track progress toward specific financial objectives, such as saving for a vacation, purchasing a home, or building an emergency fund. By allocating funds toward these goals, you can systematically work toward achieving them.

3. Provides Control Over Finances
With a budget, you gain a comprehensive understanding of your financial situation, enabling you to make informed decisions about spending and saving. This control helps prevent overspending and encourages responsible financial habits.

4. Prepares for Emergencies

A well-structured budget includes provisions for unexpected expenses, such as medical bills or car repairs. By planning for these contingencies, you can avoid financial setbacks and maintain stability during unforeseen events.

5. Promotes Financial Stability

Consistent budgeting fosters habits that lead to long-term financial stability, including regular saving and prudent spending. This stability provides peace of mind and a solid foundation for future financial endeavors.

Incorporating budgeting into your financial routine empowers you to take charge of your finances, reduce stress, and work toward your financial aspirations with confidence.

__Budgeting is often seen as a limiting process, but it is truly a tool for empowerment. This introduction highlights how mastering budgeting can change your financial life for the better.__

Chapter 1:
Facing Your Financial Reality

Understanding the Impact of Financial Stress

Relatable Scenario of Financial Stress

Imagine it's the final week of the month. Your bank account is nearing empty, and the credit card bill is looming large. The weight of uncertainty about how you'll cover your bills and still manage everyday expenses starts to sink in. This scenario is all too common, highlighting the pervasive nature of financial stress.

Broader Effects of Financial Strain

Financial stress extends beyond monetary concerns, impacting various aspects of life:

- **Mental Health Issues**: Chronic financial strain is linked to increased risks of depression, anxiety, and other mental health disorders. A study found that individuals facing financial difficulties are 4.2 times more likely to continue experiencing depression 18 months later compared to those without financial stress. Money and Mental Health
- **Strained Relationships**: Financial worries can lead to conflicts within relationships, affecting communication and intimacy. Research indicates that financial stress has a significant influence on individual and relational well-being, potentially leading to lower levels of physical and mental health. LeBaron Black
- **Poor Decision-Making**: Financial insecurity can impair cognitive functions, leading to poor decision-making. Individuals under financial stress may experience difficulties concentrating and making sound judgments, which can exacerbate financial problems. FinHealth Network

Prevalence of Financial Insecurity

Financial insecurity is a widespread issue affecting many individuals:

- **Gen Z Challenges**: A study revealed that 38% of individuals under 27 feel trapped by financial instability, job stress, and mental health issues, impacting both personal and professional aspects of their lives. New York Post
- **Economic Insecurity and Mental Health**: Research indicates that individuals with the lowest incomes are 1.5 to 3 times more likely to experience mental health issues, such as depression and anxiety, compared to higher-income individuals in the same area. FinHealth Network

These findings underscore the significant impact of financial stress on mental health, relationships, and decision-making, highlighting the importance of addressing financial insecurity to improve overall well-being.

Taking Stock of Your Current Situation

Listing All Income Sources

Understanding your full financial picture starts with identifying every source of income. This step ensures your budget is accurate and reflects all the resources you have to work with.

1. Categorize Income Sources

- **Fixed Income:**
    - Salary or wages from full-time or part-time employment.
    - Recurring income from pensions, Social Security, or annuities.
- **Variable Income:**
    - Freelance projects or contract work.
    - Side businesses or gigs (e.g., ridesharing, online sales).
    - Commissions, bonuses, or tips.
- **Passive Income:**
    - Investments: dividends, interest, or rental property income.
    - Royalties from creative work or intellectual property.

2. Steps to Calculate Total Monthly Income

1. **Collect Recent Pay Stubs or Statements:**
    a. Use at least three months of data to account for fluctuations.
2. **Estimate Irregular Income:**
    a. Use conservative averages for variable sources.
    b. For side hustles or gigs, calculate the average income from previous months.
3. **List All Sources in One Place:**
    a. Use a spreadsheet or budgeting app to compile a complete income summary.

3. Example: Monthly Income Summary

Income Source	Type	Monthly Amount
Full-Time Salary	Fixed	$4,000
Freelance Graphic Design	Variable	$500
Investment Dividends	Passive	$200
Online Store Profits	Variable	$300
TOTAL		$5,000

Tracking Expenses for 30 Days

Tracking expenses is a powerful way to uncover where your money is going and to identify habits that may be holding you back.

1. Tools for Expense Tracking

- **Budgeting Apps:**
    - **YNAB:** Offers real-time tracking and category adjustments.
    - **Mint:** Automatically categorizes transactions and tracks trends.
    - **EveryDollar:** Focused on simple, zero-based budgeting.
- **Spreadsheets:**
    - Use pre-designed templates available in Excel or Google Sheets.
    - Create categories for fixed expenses, variable expenses, and irregular costs.
- **Manual Methods:**
    - Keep a spending journal and record every purchase.

- o Use envelopes with cash for specific categories to limit spending.

2. Process for 30-Day Expense Tracking

1. **Commitment to Tracking Every Dollar:**
   a. Include all purchases, even small ones like coffee or snacks.
2. **Categorize Spending:**
   a. Use categories like housing, transportation, groceries, entertainment, and miscellaneous.
3. **Review Weekly:**
   a. Identify trends and unexpected patterns.

3. Insights Gained from Expense Tracking

Case Study: Jessica's Eye-Opening Month

Jessica, a young professional, thought her biggest expenses were rent and groceries. After tracking her spending for 30 days using Mint, she discovered she was spending over $300/month on coffee and takeout lunches. By switching to home-brewed coffee and meal prepping, she freed up $200/month to pay off her credit card debt.

Example: Mark and Emily's Budget Revelation

A couple used a spreadsheet to track their household expenses. They realized their monthly streaming subscriptions were costing $75, as they had forgotten about unused services. Canceling those subscriptions allowed them to redirect funds into their vacation savings account.

Why Tracking Expenses Matters

- **Uncovers Hidden Costs:** Identify small purchases that add up over time.
- **Empowers Decision-Making:** Prioritize spending that aligns with your values and goals.
- **Builds Financial Awareness:** Helps you stay proactive in managing your money.

By listing all income sources and tracking every dollar spent for a month, you can establish a clear financial baseline to create a sustainable budget and achieve their goals.

Acknowledging the Problem Without Shame

Experiencing financial challenges is a common aspect of life, and it's essential to approach these situations with self-compassion and a mindset geared toward improvement. Recognizing that financial struggles are a starting point for positive change can empower you to take initiative-taking steps toward financial well-being.

Practicing Self-Compassion

Self-compassion involves treating yourself with kindness and understanding during difficult times, rather than self-criticism. This approach is particularly beneficial when addressing financial difficulties.

Exercise: Self-Compassion Break

1. **Acknowledge the Situation**: Recognize that you're facing a challenging financial situation.
2. **Connect with Common Humanity**: Understand that financial struggles are a shared human experience.
3. **Practice Mindfulness**: Observe your feelings without judgment.
4. **Offer Kindness to Yourself**: Speak to yourself as you would to a close friend in a similar situation.

This exercise helps in cultivating a compassionate mindset, reducing self-criticism, and fostering resilience. Positive Psychology

Reframing Negative Self-Talk About Finances

Negative self-talk can hinder financial progress. Reframing these thoughts is crucial for developing a healthier financial mindset.

Exercise: Identifying and Reframing Negative Thoughts

1. **Identify Negative Thoughts**: Pay attention to thoughts like "I'm terrible with money" or "I'll never get out of debt."
2. **Challenge the Thoughts**: Ask yourself, "Is this thought based on facts or assumptions?"
3. **Reframe the Thought**: Replace negative thoughts with positive affirmations, such as "I am learning to manage my finances better every day."
4. **Practice Regularly**: Consistently apply this process to build a more positive financial outlook.

This practice encourages a shift from self-criticism to self-empowerment, fostering a proactive approach to financial challenges. Patti Fagan

Chapter 2:
Setting the Foundation with Goals

Clarifying What You Want

- Creating a vision board is a powerful exercise to clarify your financial dreams and priorities, transforming abstract goals into tangible, visual representations. Here's a guided approach to help you embark on this journey:
- **Reflecting on Your Dreams and Priorities**
- **Identify Your Top Three Priorities**:
    - If money were no object, what are the top three things you'd focus on?
    - How would your life change if you never had to worry about money again?
- *These questions help uncover your true passions and aspirations, providing clarity on what truly matters to you.*
- **Visualize Your Ideal Life**:
    - Imagine a day in your life without financial constraints.
    - What activities would you engage in?
    - Who would you spend time with?
    - Where would you live or travel?
- *This exercise taps into your subconscious desires, offering insights into your core values and goals.*

Creating Your Financial Vision Board

- **Gather Materials**:
    - Magazines, newspapers, or printed images
    - Scissors
    - Glue stick or tape
    - A large poster board or corkboard
- **Collect Images and Words**:
    - Look for pictures, words, or phrases that resonate with your financial goals and dreams.
    - These could include images of a dream home, vacation destinations, or symbols of financial freedom.
- **Arrange and Attach**:
    - Organize your collected items on the board, grouping them by themes or timelines.
    - Once satisfied with the arrangement, glue or tape them in place.
- **Personalize and Reflect**:
    - Add personal touches like quotes, affirmations, or drawings.
    - Reflect on how each image aligns with your financial aspirations.
- **Maintaining Motivation**
    - **Display Prominently**: Place your vision board in a location where you can see it daily, such as above your desk or near your bed.
    - **Regular Reflection**: Spend a few minutes each day visualizing achieving your goals, reinforcing your commitment.

o **Update as Needed**: As your goals evolve, feel free to add, remove, or modify elements on your board to reflect your current aspirations.

By engaging in this exercise, you create a visual representation of your financial dreams, serving as a constant reminder of your goals and the steps needed to achieve them. This practice not only clarifies your priorities but also keeps you motivated and focused on your financial journey.

The Power of SMART Goals

Setting SMART (Specific, Measurable, Achievable, Relevant, Time-bound) goals is an effective strategy for achieving financial objectives, regardless of income level. Below is a breakdown of how SMART goals can be applied across different income scenarios:

Low-Income Example: Saving $500 Within Three Months by Cutting Back on Eating Out

- **Specific**: Save $500 by reducing dining out expenses.
- **Measurable**: Track savings of $500.
- **Achievable**: Assess current spending and identify areas to cut back.
- **Relevant**: Aligns with the goal of building an emergency fund.
- **Time-bound**: Achieve within three months.

Middle-Income Example: Paying Off $2,000 Credit Card Debt Within a Year While Maintaining Some Leisure Spending

- **Specific**: Pay off $2,000 credit card debt.
- **Measurable**: Eliminate $2,000 debt.
- **Achievable**: Allocate a portion of monthly income to debt repayment.
- **Relevant**: Improves financial health and credit score.
- **Time-bound**: Complete within one year.

High-Income Example: Setting Aside $10,000 Annually for Investment to Achieve Early Retirement

- **Specific**: Invest $10,000 annually.
- **Measurable**: Invest $10,000 each year.
- **Achievable**: Determine investment vehicles and risk tolerance.
- **Relevant**: Supports the goal of early retirement.
- **Time-bound**: Invest $10,000 annually.

SMART Goals Application Across Different Income Levels

Income Level	Specific Goal	Measurable Goal	Achievable Steps	Relevant Outcome	Time-bound Deadline
Low-Income	Save $500 by reducing dining out expenses	$500 saved	Cut back on eating out; prepare meals at home	Build emergency fund	3 months
Middle-Income	Pay off $2,000 credit card debt	$2,000 debt paid	Allocate $167 monthly to debt repayment; reduce leisure spending	Improve financial health and credit score	12 months
High-Income	Invest $10,000 annually for early retirement	$10,000 invested	Research investment options; consult financial advisor	Achieve early retirement	Annually

By applying the SMART framework, individuals at various income levels can set clear, actionable financial goals tailored to their circumstances, enhancing the likelihood of achieving financial success.

Aligning Goals with Personal Values

Aligning your spending with your personal values transforms budgeting from a restrictive task into a motivating and sustainable practice. When your financial decisions reflect what truly matters to you—such as travel, family, or health—you cultivate a sense of purpose and fulfillment in your financial journey.

The Power of Values-Based Budgeting

Values-based budgeting involves directing your financial resources toward areas that align with your core beliefs and passions. This approach not only enhances financial satisfaction but also promotes healthier financial habits. By focusing on what truly matters, you may find it easier to save and invest for the future, leading to improved financial well-being. M1

Stories of Individuals Achieving Financial Peace Through Values Alignment

1. **Marie: A Grandmother's Travel Dreams**
    a. *Scenario*: Marie, an active grandmother of five, desired to travel more but was concerned about her financial security.
    b. *Approach*: She restructured her budget to prioritize travel expenses, cutting back on non-essential items like dining out and entertainment.
    c. *Outcome*: By aligning her spending with her love for travel, Marie achieved financial security and embarked on her dream vacations, experiencing financial peace and fulfillment. Frugalwoods
2. **Regina Moore: Achieving Financial Independence**
    a. *Scenario*: Regina Moore, a pharmacist from rural Oregon, aimed to achieve financial independence by saving a significant portion of her income.
    b. *Approach*: She maintained a lean lifestyle, avoiding consumerism and focusing on paying off debt and investing wisely.
    c. *Outcome*: By aligning her spending with her values of financial independence and frugality, Regina saved $1 million by the age of 36, allowing her to consider a work-optional lifestyle. The Cut

Implementing Values-Based Budgeting

To align your budget with your personal values:

1. **Identify Your Core Values**: Reflect on what truly matters to you—be it travel, family, health, or other passions.
2. **Assess Current Spending**: Review your expenses to determine if they align with your identified values.
3. **Adjust Your Budget**: Reallocate funds to prioritize areas that reflect your values, reducing spending on non-essential items.
4. **Monitor and Reflect**: Regularly assess your financial decisions to ensure they continue to align with your values, making adjustments as needed.

By integrating your personal values into your budgeting process, you create a financial plan that not only supports your goals but also enhances your overall well-being and satisfaction.

Chapter 3:
Mastering the Basics of Budgeting

Budgeting Methods 101

Understanding and implementing effective budgeting methods can significantly enhance financial management and help achieve personal financial goals. Here are three popular budgeting strategies: Zero-Based Budgeting, the 50/30/20 Rule, and the Envelope Method.

1. Zero-Based Budgeting

Zero-Based Budgeting (ZBB) requires allocating every dollar of your income to a specific expense category, savings, or debt repayment, ensuring that your income minus expenditures equals zero.

How It Works:

- **Income Assessment**: Calculate your total monthly income.
- **Expense Allocation**: Assign every dollar to a category, including fixed expenses (rent, utilities), variable expenses (groceries, entertainment), savings, and debt payments.
- **Adjustments**: If expenses exceed income, identify areas to reduce spending; if there's surplus income, allocate it to savings or debt repayment.

Benefits:

- **Comprehensive Tracking**: Provides detailed insight into spending habits.
- **Intentional Spending**: Encourages deliberate allocation of funds, reducing wasteful expenditures.
- **Financial Discipline**: Promotes disciplined financial management by requiring justification for all expenses.

2. The 50/30/20 Rule

The 50/30/20 Rule is a straightforward budgeting framework that divides after-tax income into three categories:

- **50% for Needs**: Essential expenses such as housing, food, transportation, and utilities.
- **30% for Wants**: Non-essential items like dining out, hobbies, and entertainment.
- **20% for Savings and Debt Repayment**: Allocations for savings accounts, investments, and paying off debts.

How It Works:

1. **Calculate After-Tax Income**: Determine your monthly income after taxes.
2. **Apply the Percentages**:
    a. Allocate 50% to needs.
    b. Allocate 30% to wants.
    c. Allocate 20% to savings and debt repayment.
3. **Monitor and Adjust**: Regularly review spending to ensure it aligns with these percentages and make adjustments as necessary.

Benefits:

- **Simplicity**: Easy to understand and implement.
- **Flexibility**: Allows for personal spending within limits, reducing feelings of restriction.
- **Balanced Financial Health**: Ensures essential needs are met while promoting savings and manageable discretionary spending.

3. Envelope Method

The Envelope Method is a cash-based budgeting system that allocates physical cash to spending categories, helping control expenditures.

How It Works:

1. **Identify Spending Categories**: Determine categories such as groceries, dining out, transportation, etc.
2. **Allocate Cash**: Withdraw cash corresponding to the budgeted amount for each category and place it into labeled envelopes.
3. **Spend from Envelopes**: Use only the cash in each envelope for its designated purpose. Once an envelope is empty, spending in that category stops until it's replenished.

Benefits:

- **Spending Awareness**: Physically overseeing cash can increase awareness of spending habits.
- **Expenditure Control**: Limits overspending by restricting spending to the cash available.
- **Debt Avoidance**: Encourages spending within means, reducing reliance on credit.

Considerations:

- **Security**: Carrying cash can pose security risks; consider using a modified digital version if concerned.
- **Practicality**: May be less convenient in a predominantly digital payment society.

Each of these budgeting methods offers unique advantages. Choosing the right one depends on individual financial situations, spending habits, and personal preferences.

Choosing Your Starting Point

Choosing the Right Budgeting Method

Selecting a budgeting method that matches your financial situation, and personality is crucial for long-term success. The following flowchart and descriptions will guide you to the approach that works best for you.

Flowchart:
Which Budgeting Method Should You Choose?

1. **Do you have irregular income (e.g., freelancing, gig work)?**
    a. Yes → Envelope Method or Zero-Based Budgeting
    b. No → Continue
2. **Do you want to track every dollar and closely monitor spending?**
    a. Yes → Zero-Based Budgeting
    b. No → Continue
3. **Are you looking for a simple and time-efficient budgeting approach?**
    a. Yes → 50/30/20 Rule
    b. No → Continue
4. **Do you struggle with overspending in specific areas?**
    a. Yes → Envelope Method
    b. No → Consider a hybrid of methods (e.g., combining Zero-Based Budgeting with elements of the 50/30/20 Rule).

Budgeting Method Descriptions

Zero-Based Budgeting

- **Best For**: Individuals who want to allocate every dollar intentionally.
- **How It Works**: Assign all income to specific categories (expenses, savings, debt repayment) so that income minus expenses equals zero.
- **Personality Fit**: Detail-oriented individuals who enjoy planning and maintaining close control of their finances.

50/30/20 Rule

- **Best For**: Those seeking simplicity and balance in their financial management.
- **How It Works**: Allocate 50% of income to needs, 30% to wants, and 20% to savings and debt repayment.
- **Personality Fit**: Individuals who prefer a straightforward approach without extensive tracking.

Envelope Method

- **Best For**: People who want to control overspending in specific areas.
- **How It Works**: Withdraw cash for each spending category and place it in labeled envelopes. Use only the cash in each envelope for its designated purpose.
- **Personality Fit**: Those who benefit from visual and tangible spending limits.

Hybrid Methods

- **Best For**: People who want flexibility and customization.
- **How It Works**: Combine aspects of different budgeting methods to suit your unique needs. For example, use Zero-Based Budgeting for fixed expenses and the Envelope Method for discretionary spending.
- **Personality Fit**: Individuals comfortable with experimentation and adapting systems to their lifestyle.

Quiz Questions to Refine Your Choice

1. **How much time can you dedicate to budgeting each week?**
   - ☐ Less than 30 minutes: 50/30/20 Rule
   - ☐ More than 30 minutes: Zero-Based Budgeting or Envelope Method
2. **Do you prefer using cash or digital tools for budgeting?**
   - ☐ Cash: Envelope Method
   - ☐ Digital tools: Zero-Based Budgeting or 50/30/20 Rule
3. **Are you motivated by detailed tracking or simplicity?**
   - ☐ Detailed tracking: Zero-Based Budgeting
   - ☐ Simplicity: 50/30/20 Rule
4. **Do you have difficulty sticking to spending limits in certain categories?**
   - ☐ Yes: Envelope Method
   - ☐ No: Any method

Final Tips

- **Experiment**: It's okay to try a method and switch if it doesn't work. Budgeting is a personal process.
- **Combine Methods**: Don't hesitate to mix and match strategies to create a system that suits you.
- **Stay Consistent**: No matter which method you choose, regular tracking and adjustments are key to success.

Setting Up Your First Budget

Clear Templates and Step-by-Step Instructions

Step-by-Step Guide to Creating Your First Budget

1. **Gather Financial Information**:
    a. Collect your income details, recent bank statements, and bills.
    b. Note irregular income sources and variable expenses.
2. **Calculate Your Total Income**:
    a. Include all sources of income (e.g., salary, freelance work, side hustles).
3. **List Your Expenses**:
    a. Divide expenses into fixed (e.g., rent, insurance) and variable (e.g., groceries, entertainment).
    b. Don't forget irregular expenses (e.g., annual subscriptions, car maintenance).
4. **Choose a Budgeting Method**:
    a. Refer to the flowchart and method descriptions above to select the best approach.
5. **Allocate Your Income**:
    a. Assign specific amounts to each category. Use tools like spreadsheets, apps, or templates to stay organized.
6. **Track Spending**:
    a. Monitor expenses daily or weekly to ensure adherence to your budget.
7. **Adjust as Needed**:
    a. Review your budget monthly and make adjustments for unexpected changes or errors.

Budget Template Example

Category	Budgeted Amount	Actual Amount	Difference
Income	$3,000		
Rent/Mortgage	$1,000		
Utilities	$200		
Groceries	$400		
Transportation	$150		
Savings	$600		
Entertainment	$150		
Other Expenses	$500		

Troubleshooting Common Mistakes

1. **Forgetting Irregular Expenses**:
    a. **Solution**: Create a "sinking fund" for irregular costs by setting aside a small amount each month.
    b. Example: Divide a $1,200 annual car maintenance cost into $100 monthly savings.
2. **Overestimating Income**:
    a. **Solution**: Base your budget on average income or the lowest recent month's earnings to avoid shortfalls.
3. **Underestimating Expenses**:
    a. **Solution**: Track expenses for a month to understand actual spending habits before finalizing your budget.
4. **Not Updating the Budget Regularly**:
    a. **Solution**: Schedule a monthly review to adjust for changes in income or expenses.
5. **Feeling Overwhelmed**:
    a. **Solution**: Start with a simple method like the 50/30/20 Rule, then transition to detailed tracking as you gain confidence.

Chapter 4:
Tracking and Adjusting

The Importance of Tracking Expenses

Consistent tracking of your finances is essential for achieving financial success. By diligently monitoring income and expenses, you gain a clear understanding of your financial habits, enabling informed decisions and effective budgeting. This practice helps identify areas where you can reduce spending, allocate funds more efficiently, and work toward financial goals. Moreover, regular tracking can prevent debt accumulation and enhance your ability to manage unexpected expenses. Experian

To assist with financial tracking, consider the following popular tools:

>You Need A Budget (YNAB)
>Mint
>Excel

Many individuals have transformed their financial lives through diligent tracking. For example:

- **Liz and her husband**: By consistently budgeting, they paid off over $180,000 in just five years, despite not having an excessive income. You Need A Budget
- **Janis**: Utilizing the 'envelope trick' for budgeting, she managed her expenses effectively, leading to extra savings and eventually purchasing her first home. UW Story

These success stories highlight the profound impact that consistent financial tracking can have, leading to debt reduction, increased savings, and the achievement of significant financial milestones.

Analyzing Spending Patterns

Exercises to Identify Spending Patterns

Step 1: Gather Your Data

- Collect financial statements (bank, credit card) for the last 1-3 months.
- Use a highlighter or create a spreadsheet to categorize each expense (e.g., subscriptions, dining, groceries, shopping).

Step 2: Look for Recurring Expenses

- Identify recurring subscriptions: streaming services, gym memberships, meal kits, etc.
- Ask yourself:
    - Do I still use this service regularly?
    - Can I switch to a lower-cost or free alternative?

Example:

- **Expense:** A $14.99 subscription to a premium app.
- **Action:** Cancel or switch to the free version if usage is minimal.

Step 3:
Spot Impulsive Purchases

- Mark purchases that weren't planned or budgeted.
- Reflect on what triggered these buys (e.g., sales, emotions, boredom).
- Group these by type to find trends (e.g., online shopping, dining out).

Step 4:
Analyze Spending by Category

- Calculate the percentage of total income spent on each category.
- Compare it to recommended guidelines (e.g., 50/30/20 rule: 50% needs, 30% wants, 20% savings/debt).

Suggested Tools for Spending Analysis

1. **Apps for Automated Categorization**
   a. **Mint:** Automatically groups expenses and tracks recurring charges.
   b. **YNAB (You Need A Budget):** Helps you review spending habits and align with goals.
2. **Excel or Google Sheets**
   a. Use templates to manually input expenses, making patterns easy to spot.
   b. Include formulas to calculate totals and percentages.
3. **Banking Apps**
   a. Many banks provide built-in spending analysis features.

Adjusting Habits Based on Analysis

1. **Reduce Recurring Costs:**
    a. Cancel unused subscriptions or negotiate for better rates.
    b. Set reminders to reevaluate subscriptions every 3-6 months.
2. **Control Impulse Spending:**
    a. Use a "cooling-off" period before purchases over $50.
    b. Remove stored payment methods from online shopping accounts to make purchases less convenient.
3. **Reallocate Funds to Align with Goals:**
    a. Redirect funds saved from unnecessary expenses to savings or debt repayment.
    b. For example, save $40/month from canceled subscriptions to build an emergency fund.

Exercise:
Spending Habit Reflection

1. **Daily Tracking:** For 7 days, note every purchase in real-time.
    a. At the end of the week, review for patterns (e.g., frequent coffee runs).
2. **Habit Journal:** Reflect on emotional states before and after purchases.
    a. **Example:** "I bought a new jacket after a stressful meeting."
    b. Plan alternative responses for future triggers (e.g., take a walk instead of shopping).

By engaging in these exercises and using tools effectively, you can uncover spending habits, adjust them, and align their finances with their goals.

Adapting as You Go

Preparing for Financial Setbacks or Changes

Life is unpredictable, and significant events like job loss, having a baby, or unexpected medical expenses can challenge even the most robust budgets. Preparation and adaptability are key to navigating these transitions smoothly.

Step 1:
Build a Financial Safety Net

1. **Emergency Fund:**
    a. Aim to save 3–6 months of living expenses.
    b. Start small: set an initial goal of $500–$1,000.
    c. Automate savings contributions to make this goal achievable.
2. **Insurance Coverage:**
    a. Review and update health, disability, and life insurance policies.
    b. Ensure coverage is adequate to manage potential emergencies.
3. **Debt Management Plan:**
    a. Pay down high-interest debt to free up cash flow for unexpected expenses.
    b. Explore debt consolidation options to lower monthly payments if necessary.

Step 2:
Adjusting Budgets During Major Life Changes

Scenario 1: Job Loss

- **Immediate Steps:**
    - Prioritize essentials (housing, utilities, food, and insurance).
    - Pause discretionary spending like dining out, subscriptions, and travel.
    - Notify creditors to discuss hardship options (e.g., deferred payments).
- **Budget Adjustments:**
    - Shift focus to living on unemployment benefits or savings.
    - Reallocate non-essential categories to critical areas.

Scenario 2:
Having a Baby

- **Anticipate New Expenses:**
    - Hospital bills, childcare, diapers, and baby supplies.
    - Research childcare options and costs in advance.
- **Budget Adjustments:**
    - Increase savings for upfront costs (crib, car seat, etc.).
    - Create a category for recurring baby-related expenses.
- **Long-Term Planning:**
    - Open a 529 plan or savings account for education costs.
    - Reassess health insurance plans for better coverage.

Scenario 3:
Facing Unexpected Expenses

- **Emergency Response:**
    - Tap into the emergency fund as a first line of defense.
    - Use credit only as a last resort and have a repayment plan.
- **Budget Adjustments:**
    - Temporarily reduce spending in non-essential categories.
    - Consider picking up a side hustle or selling unused items to offset costs.

Step 3:
Maintain Flexibility

1. **Revaluate Budget Regularly:**
    a. Schedule monthly reviews to adjust for changes in income or expenses.
    b. Identify areas where cuts can be made during lean months.
2. **Adopt a Variable Income Budget:**
    a. If income is irregular (freelancers, gig workers), base budgets on the lowest average monthly income.
    b. Save surplus earnings during high-income months for lean periods.
3. **Create a Contingency Plan:**
    a. Document steps to take during financial disruptions, such as reducing spending, reaching out for financial assistance, or finding temporary work.

Mental Resilience During Setbacks

- Practice self-compassion and focus on what you can control.
- Seek support from friends, family, or financial advisors.
- Remember that financial setbacks are temporary and can be overcome with persistence and planning.

By preparing ahead and maintaining a flexible approach, you can face life's uncertainties with greater confidence and control over their finances.

Chapter 5: Overcoming Common Challenges

Breaking the Cycle of Overspending

Strategies for Avoiding Overspending

Overspending can derail even the best budgeting efforts. By identifying triggers, implementing practical limits, and building mindful habits, you can regain control over your finances.

1. Identify Your Spending Triggers

Reflect on Emotional Triggers:

- **Common Patterns:**
    - Shopping as a response to stress, boredom, or celebrations.
    - Purchasing items to boost self-esteem or "keep up" with peers.
- **Action Plan:**
    - Keep a spending journal: Log how you feel before and after each discretionary purchase.
    - Replace shopping with healthier coping strategies, like exercising, journaling, or calling a friend.

Analyze Situational Triggers:

- **Examples:**
    - Browsing online sales, window shopping, or impulsive buys during errands.
    - Peer pressure during social outings (e.g., group dinners or trips).
- **Action Plan:**
    - Avoid temptation: Stay away from "browsing" environments unless you're shopping with a purpose.
    - Prepare for social events: Set a spending cap or suggest budget-friendly activities.

2. Avoid Impulse Purchases

Implement a Cooling-Off Period:

- **The 24-Hour Rule:** Wait at least one day before making non-essential purchases.
- **Wish List Approach:** Add items to a wish list or cart and revisit after a week to reassess your interest.

Limit Instant Gratification:

- Remove stored payment methods from online accounts to make purchases less convenient.
- Disable "one-click" purchasing options on platforms like Amazon.

3. Set Spending Limits

Create Budget Caps for Discretionary Categories:

- Example: Allocate $100/month for dining out or $50/month for hobbies.
- Track spending in real time with apps like YNAB, Mint, or custom spreadsheets.

Use Cash for Discretionary Spending:

- Withdraw a predetermined amount for categories like entertainment or shopping.
- Once the cash is gone, the spending stops.

4. Reduce Exposure to Temptation

Unsubscribe from Retail Emails and Notifications:

- Retailers use promotions and sales to create a false sense of urgency.
- Use apps like **Unroll.me** to unsubscribe from multiple lists simultaneously.

Declutter Marketing Influences:

- Install ad blockers or use browser extensions to reduce exposure to targeted ads.
- Unfollow social media accounts that encourage excessive spending.

5. Build Conscious Spending Habits

Shop with a Purpose:

- Make a list before entering stores or shopping online.
- Stick to the list, avoiding unplanned purchases.

Reframe Spending Decisions:

- Before buying, ask:
    - "Do I really need this?"
    - "How does this purchase align with my goals and values?"

Reward Yourself Without Spending:

- Celebrate achievements (e.g., sticking to your budget) with free or low-cost activities, like a relaxing evening or a DIY project.

6. Leverage Tools for Overspending Prevention

Budgeting Apps with Alerts:

- Use apps that send notifications when you approach category limits.
- Example: YNAB encourages reallocation when overspending occurs.

Prepaid Cards or Gift Cards:

- Load a set amount for specific categories, limiting spending to the preloaded balance.

Case Study: Maria's Journey to Controlled Spending

Maria realized she often overspent on online shopping during stressful workdays. By unsubscribing from retail emails and implementing a 24-hour rule, she reduced unnecessary purchases by 40%. She now uses a budgeting app to track her discretionary spending and celebrates sticking to her limits with a family game night.

With these strategies, you can proactively manage their spending, reduce financial stress, and focus on reaching their long-term goals.

Dealing with Irregular Income

Strategies for Managing Inconsistent Income

Freelancers, seasonal workers, and those with variable income face unique challenges when budgeting. By implementing these strategies, they can create financial stability even during lean months.

1. Build a Financial Buffer During High-Earning Months

Why It's Important

A financial buffer ensures you can cover expenses when income dips. It acts as a personal safety net, reducing stress and reliance on credit.

How to Do It

1. **Calculate a Baseline Monthly Expense:**
    a. Identify essential expenses like rent, utilities, groceries, and insurance.
    b. Use past bills and receipts to determine the minimum you need to get by.
2. **Create a High-Income Savings Plan:**
    a. Save a fixed percentage (e.g., 30%-50%) of your income during peak months.
    b. Deposit this into a separate high-yield savings account to discourage unnecessary spending.

3. **Prioritize Buffer Goals:**
    a. Aim to save 3–6 months' worth of baseline expenses as a cushion.
    b. Focus on building this before discretionary spending or aggressive debt repayment.

2. Use a "Pay Yourself First" Approach

What It Means

Before paying bills or spending on wants, allocate a portion of your income to savings or an emergency fund.

How It Helps

This ensures that saving becomes a priority, not an afterthought, even during higher-earning periods.

3. Base Budgets on Average Income, Not Peaks

Step-by-Step Process

1. **Determine Your Average Income:**
    a. Calculate the average of your income over 6–12 months to smooth out fluctuations.
2. **Plan Around the Lowest Average:**
    a. Build your budget based on the lowest income month in that period.
    b. Any excess income during high-earning months can be directed to savings or buffers.

Example:

Month	Income	Action Taken During High-Income Months
January	$3,500	Save $1,000 for leaner months
February	$4,200	Save $1,500
March	$2,800	Use saved buffer to supplement expenses

4. Set Up Separate Accounts for Budget Categories

- **Operating Account:** For regular monthly expenses.
- **Savings Account:** For emergency funds and buffers.
- **Seasonal Needs Fund:** For irregular expenses like holiday gifts or travel.

Using multiple accounts can help you stay organized and resist the temptation to overspend.

5. Use Variable Income to Plan Ahead

Plan for Big Expenses:

- During peak earning periods, allocate money for predictable future costs, such as taxes, insurance premiums, or annual subscriptions.

Automate Savings for Long-Term Goals:

- Automate transfers to retirement accounts or investments during high-earning months to maintain progress toward financial goals.

6. Maintain Flexibility in Your Budget

Adjust Categories Monthly:

- Track spending and reallocate funds to where they're needed most.

Example Adjustment:

- If unexpected medical bills arise, reduce discretionary spending categories like dining out or entertainment.

Case Study: Maria the Freelancer

Maria works as a graphic designer, earning $2,000 in some months and up to $5,000 in others. To stabilize her finances, she:

1. **Built a $10,000 Buffer:** Saved aggressively during a period of high client demand.
2. **Automated Her Savings:** Allocated 40% of each paycheck into a high-yield savings account.
3. **Budgeted Conservatively:** Based her monthly expenses on her lowest income months.
4. **Adapted to Changes:** Used a detailed spreadsheet to adjust her budget as needed.

With these strategies, Maria avoided debt during slower months and maintained peace of mind.

By building financial buffers, automating savings, and adopting a flexible approach, individuals with irregular income can navigate financial uncertainty with confidence.

Managing Setbacks Without Guilt

Handling financial setbacks gracefully is an important skill that can help you grow, stay resilient, and ultimately build a stronger financial future. Setbacks are a natural part of life, but it's how you handle them that determines your success. Rather than letting guilt take over, focus on learning from the experience and taking proactive steps to get back on track.

1. Acknowledge Your Feelings Without Guilt

Financial setbacks can evoke strong emotions, stress, frustration, disappointment, or even guilt. It's essential to acknowledge these emotions, but don't let guilt take over. Remember, no one is perfect, and mistakes are part of the journey. Instead of feeling ashamed, use this moment to reflect and learn.

"The only real mistake is the one from which we learn nothing." – Henry Ford

Guilt will only hold you back from moving forward. Release it and focus on what you can do now to move in a positive direction.

2. Shift Your Mindset from Guilt to Growth

A mindset shift is key. Instead of dwelling on what went wrong, embrace the setback as an opportunity for growth. Every financial challenge offers valuable lessons that can help you make wiser choices in the future.

"Success is not final, failure is not fatal: It is the courage to continue that counts." – Winston Churchill

This quote reminds you that failure is not the end, but rather a chance to keep pushing forward. Use setbacks as steppingstones to build a stronger financial foundation.

3. Create a Clear Plan for Recovery

Once you've accepted the setback and reframed it as a learning opportunity, it's time to act. Break down the steps needed to recover. Focus on what you can control, such as budgeting, saving, and cutting unnecessary expenses. Creating a clear plan will help you regain control of your finances.

"The way to get started is to quit talking and begin doing." – Walt Disney

Focus on taking small, manageable steps toward your goal. It's not about immediate perfection but consistent progress.

4. Seek Support and Guidance

Financial setbacks can feel isolating, but you're not alone. Seeking support from family, friends, or even a financial advisor can provide fresh perspectives and practical advice. There are many who have faced similar challenges and can offer guidance.

"Alone we can do so little; together we can do so much." – Helen Keller

Don't hesitate to reach out for help. Sometimes, the right advice or support can make all the difference.

5. Practice Patience and Self-Compassion

Healing from a financial setback takes time. Be patient with yourself and remember that growth doesn't happen overnight. Celebrate small victories along the way, and don't rush the process.

"Patience is not the ability to wait, but how you act while you're waiting." – Joyce Meyer

Trust that, with time and effort, you'll emerge from this setback stronger and wiser. Allow yourself to be kind and patient with your progress.

6. Develop Preventative Measures for the Future

Once you've learned from the experience, consider what measures you can put in place to avoid similar issues in the future. This might involve better budgeting practices, creating an emergency fund, or learning about investing. By proactively setting yourself up for success, you increase your financial resilience.

"By failing to prepare, you are preparing to fail." – Benjamin Franklin

Preparation is key to preventing future setbacks and ensuring you're in a better position moving forward.

7. Stay Focused on Your Long-Term Goals

Finally, remember that a single financial setback does not define your future. It's a small chapter in your larger financial story. Keep your eyes on your long-term goals and stay committed to improving your financial health. Use affirmations to stay motivated and remind yourself that setbacks are temporary.

Affirmations for Financial Resilience:

- "I learn from my mistakes and grow stronger each day."
- "Every setback is an opportunity to improve and get closer to my goals."
- "I am capable of turning my financial situation around."

- "I am in control of my financial future, and I am taking the right steps toward success."
- "I trust in my ability to recover and build a prosperous life."

Final Thought: Keep Moving Forward

Life is full of ups and downs, but how you handle those moments determines your success. Rather than getting bogged down by guilt, focus on the lessons learned from your financial setback. Use your challenges to fuel your growth,

develop your resilience, and build a stronger, more secure financial future.

"The journey of a thousand miles begins with one step." – Lao Tzu

Every small step you take today brings you closer to a brighter financial future. Keep moving forward with confidence, knowing that you are capable of achieving your long-term goals.

Chapter 6:
Building Savings and Security

Starting Small, Thinking Big

Starting small with a manageable emergency fund is one of the best ways to lay a strong financial foundation. It can feel overwhelming to think about large savings goals, especially if you're just starting or dealing with financial setbacks. However, breaking the process down into smaller, achievable milestones helps build confidence, motivation, and momentum for future financial goals.

1. Start with a Manageable Emergency Fund

An emergency fund is essential for protecting yourself from unexpected financial hardships, such as medical bills, car repairs, or job loss. Starting small is not only practical, it also helps you build the habit of saving regularly without feeling overwhelmed.

Begin with a target that's achievable, like $500 to $1,000. This may seem modest, but it's a realistic amount that can help you weather smaller emergencies. Once this initial goal is met, you'll gain the confidence to save even more.

"The journey of a thousand miles begins with one step." – **Lao Tzu**

Just like any journey, the key is to take that first step. When you hit your first small milestone, you'll realize that saving for bigger goals is possible and that you have the ability to achieve them.

2. Build Confidence with Small Wins

Small savings goals are less intimidating and easier to attain, especially when you're starting from scratch. When you set a goal that's within reach, and you achieve it, you'll feel a sense of accomplishment. This creates a positive feedback loop—confidence in your ability to save grows, which encourages you to continue making progress.

"Success is the sum of small efforts, repeated day in and day out." – **Robert Collier**

As you hit these smaller milestones, you'll gain experience, discipline, and confidence in your financial habits. Each win, no matter how small, will give you the motivation to continue working toward bigger savings goals.

3. The Power of Consistency

One of the most powerful aspects of starting small is consistency. By setting a manageable emergency fund goal, you avoid the temptation to take on unrealistic savings targets that could lead to burnout or discouragement. When you break it down into small, steady contributions, you begin to form a sustainable habit of saving.

"The secret to getting ahead is getting started." **– Mark Twain**

Even if you're only able to save a small amount each week or month, consistency over time is what ultimately leads to larger savings. The key is to start where you are and commit to making regular contributions.

4. Building Momentum for Larger Goals

Once your initial emergency fund is in place, you'll have built the confidence and discipline needed to tackle larger financial goals, such as saving for a down payment on a house, building a retirement fund, or paying off debt. Starting small helps create a solid financial habit, which is the foundation for meeting bigger milestones.

As you progress, consider gradually increasing your savings rate. Maybe you start by saving $50 or $100 a month and, over time, increase it as your financial situation improves. The success of hitting smaller milestones will inspire you to keep going.

"A goal without a plan is just a wish." **– Antoine de Saint-Exupéry**

By setting small, specific goals, you're making sure your plans are actionable. And as you achieve these smaller goals, you'll be that much closer to accomplishing larger ones.

5. Celebrate Your Progress

Celebrating your small victories is crucial. Each milestone you hit is an achievement, and taking the time to acknowledge your progress helps reinforce the habit of saving. You don't need to throw a big party, but taking a moment to appreciate your effort can keep you motivated to continue working toward your next goal.

"The way to get started is to quit talking and begin doing." – **Walt Disney**

Taking action, no matter how small, is the key to financial success. Celebrate every little step you take toward building your financial future.

6. Set Up for Long-Term Success

Once you've created a manageable emergency fund, the next step is to set even larger goals—whether it's paying off credit card debt, saving for retirement, or building a more substantial emergency fund. However, this is only possible if you've first mastered the art of saving small, consistent amounts. The discipline and confidence gained from these small victories will empower you to pursue bigger goals without feeling overwhelmed.

"The best way to predict the future is to create it." – **Abraham Lincoln**

When you start small, you're laying the groundwork for long-term financial success. The habits you build today will serve as the steppingstones to achieving your larger financial dreams.

Final Thought: Small Steps, Big Results

By starting small, you allow yourself the time and space to build healthy financial habits. Each small step brings you closer to your larger financial goals. Whether it's creating an emergency fund, saving for a big purchase, or securing your retirement, starting with small, manageable milestones will help you build the confidence needed to tackle bigger goals with ease. The key is consistency, patience, and understanding that every step forward, no matter how small, progress is.

"Do not wait; the time will never be 'just right.'" – **Napoleon Hill**

Start today, take that first small step, and watch how your financial journey unfolds!

The Importance of Automation

Setting up automatic transfers to your savings account is one of the best ways to make saving money effortless and consistent. By automating your savings, you ensure that you pay yourself first, without the temptation to spend money before saving it. Here's a step-by-step guide on how to set it up, along with tools and apps that can help you reach your savings goals faster.

1. Choose the Right Savings Account

Before you set up automatic transfers, it's important to choose the right savings account. For your hard-earned money to grow faster, consider opening a **high-yield savings account (HYSA)**. These accounts typically offer higher interest rates than traditional savings accounts, allowing your money to grow faster over time.

Why High-Yield Savings Accounts?

- **Higher Interest Rates**: They generally offer 10 to 25 times higher interest rates than standard savings accounts.
- **Safety**: They're typically FDIC insured, meaning your money is protected up to $250,000.
- **Accessibility**: You can easily access your funds when needed, although some accounts may have limited withdrawals.

Recommended High-Yield Savings Accounts:

- **Ally Bank**: Known for its competitive rates and no monthly fees.
- **Marcus by Goldman Sachs**: Offers high interest with no fees or minimums.

- **Discover Bank**: Provides a great online savings experience with no fees.

2. Set Up Automatic Transfers with Your Bank

Most banks, whether traditional or online, offer easy ways to set up automatic transfers from your checking account to your savings account. This process will vary slightly depending on the bank, but here's a general guide:

1. **Log in to Your Bank Account**: Access your online banking through your bank's website or mobile app.
2. **Navigate to Transfers or Payments**: Look for the section where you can set up recurring transfers or scheduled payments.
3. **Choose the Accounts**: Select your checking account as the "from" account and your savings account as the "to" account.
4. **Set the Amount and Frequency**: Choose how much money you want to transfer and how often (e.g., weekly, bi-weekly, monthly).
5. **Review and Confirm**: Double-check the details, then confirm the transfer schedule.

3. Use Apps to Automate Saving

In addition to setting up automatic transfers with your bank, there are several apps designed specifically to help you save money automatically. These apps can round up your purchases to the nearest dollar or set aside a percentage of your income to transfer to savings.

Recommended Apps for Automating Savings:

- **Qapital**: This app allows you to create different savings goals (vacation, emergency fund, etc.) and set up automatic transfers. You can also enable the "Round-Up" feature, where your purchases are rounded up to the nearest dollar and the difference is saved.

- **Digit**: Digit analyzes your spending habits and automatically transfers small amounts of money from your checking account into your Digit savings account. It's a great option for those who want to save without thinking about it.
- **Chime**: Chime offers a feature called **Save When I Get Paid**, which automatically moves 10% of each direct deposit payment into a separate savings account.
- **Simple**: Simple has a "Goals" feature that lets you set up automatic transfers for specific goals like emergency funds or travel. It also offers a "Safe-to-Spend" feature, helping you budget for your goals by showing how much money you have available to spend after factoring in your savings.

4. Start Small and Gradually Increase Transfers

If you're new to saving automatically, start small. Set up an automatic transfer for a manageable amount, like $25 or $50 per week. Over time, as your budget allows, increase this amount. The key is consistency and making sure the amount is sustainable, so you don't find it difficult to stick with.

Tip: The "set it and forget it" approach works best when you forget about the transfers entirely, making them automatic and seamless.

5. Set Up Multiple Savings Goals

Many apps and banks allow you to set up multiple savings goals simultaneously. For example, you could set one account for an emergency fund, another for vacation savings, and another for a down payment on a house. This can be motivating, as you can see your money working toward different objectives.

6. Monitor and Adjust Your Transfers

Once you've set up automatic transfers, it's a good idea to review your progress periodically. Check how your savings are growing and adjust the amount if needed. If you receive a raise or find extra money in your budget, consider increasing your transfers. On the other hand, if you need to cut back, it's okay to adjust temporarily—just make sure to stay consistent.

7. Use Alerts and Notifications

Many banks and apps offer notifications to let you know when a transfer has been made or when you've reached a certain savings goal. These alerts can help you stay on track and motivated to keep saving.

Final Thought: Making Saving Easy and Automatic

By setting up automatic transfers, you take the guesswork and temptation out of saving. Whether you use your bank's built-in features or apps designed for automatic saving, you can watch your savings grow with little effort on your part. The key is consistency and making the process as automatic as paying your monthly bills. By starting small, using high-yield savings accounts, and utilizing helpful apps, you'll be well on your way to reaching your financial goals with ease.

"The habit of saving is one of the most powerful tools you can use to create financial security." **– Suze Orman**

Planning for the Future

Planning for retirement is a crucial step toward ensuring financial security in your later years. By understanding and utilizing retirement accounts like Individual Retirement Accounts (IRAs) and 401(k) plans, you can build wealth and enjoy a comfortable retirement. Here's a guide to help you get started with retirement planning and investing.

1. Understand Retirement Accounts

- **Individual Retirement Accounts (IRAs):** IRAs are personal accounts that offer tax advantages to encourage retirement savings. There are two main types:
  - **Traditional IRA:** Contributions may be tax-deductible, and earnings grow tax-deferred until withdrawal. Withdrawals in retirement are taxed as ordinary income.
  - **Roth IRA:** Contributions are made with after-tax dollars, but qualified withdrawals in retirement are tax-free. This is beneficial if you anticipate being in a higher tax bracket during retirement.
- **401(k) Plans:** Offered by employers, 401(k) plans allow you to contribute a portion of your salary before taxes. Many employers offer matching contributions, which is essentially free money to boost your retirement savings. Some employers also offer Roth 401(k) options, combining features of both Traditional and Roth IRAs.

2. Determine How Much to Save

Assess your current expenses and estimate how much income you'll need in retirement. Financial advisors often recommend aiming to replace 70-80% of your pre-retirement income. Tools like retirement calculators can help estimate the amount you need to save based on your desired retirement age and lifestyle.

3. Start Early and Contribute Regularly

The earlier you start saving, the more time your investments must grow, thanks to compound interest. Even small, consistent contributions can accumulate significantly over time. Automating your contributions can help maintain consistency.

4. Diversify Your Investments

Diversification involves spreading your investments across various asset classes (stocks, bonds, real estate) to manage risk. Consider a mix of investments that align with your risk tolerance and time horizon. As you approach retirement, you might gradually shift toward more conservative investments to preserve capital.

5. Take Advantage of Employer-Sponsored Plans

If your employer offers a 401(k) plan with matching contributions, aim to contribute at least enough to receive the full match. This is essentially additional compensation and can significantly boost your retirement savings.

6. Consider Professional Advice

Consulting with a financial advisor can provide personalized guidance based on your financial situation and retirement goals. They can help you develop a comprehensive retirement plan and assist with investment strategies.

7. Stay Informed and Review Regularly

Regularly reviewing your retirement plan ensures it remains aligned with your goals and adapts to any life changes. Stay informed about changes in tax laws, contribution limits, and investment options to make informed decisions.

Motivational Quote:

"The best time to plant a tree was 20 years ago. The second best time is now." — **Chinese Proverb**

Starting your retirement planning today, regardless of your age, is a proactive step toward securing your financial future.

By understanding retirement accounts, setting clear savings goals, and consistently contributing to your retirement funds, you can build a solid foundation for a comfortable and financially secure retirement.

Chapter 7:
Creating Long-Term Financial Habits

Reinforcing Positive Behaviors

Celebrating small financial victories is essential for maintaining motivation and reinforcing positive financial habits. Acknowledging achievements like paying off a debt or adhering to a budget for a month not only boosts morale but also propels you toward your long-term financial goals.

The Importance of Celebrating Small Financial Wins

Recognizing and celebrating minor financial successes can significantly impact your financial journey. According to Faster Capital, celebrating small wins boosts confidence and creates momentum, making it more likely to continue on the path to financial success. FasterCapital

Similarly, Utah First Credit Union emphasizes that even small wins can boost emotions and motivation, leading to greater success in financial endeavors. Utah First

Non-Financial Rewards to Reinforce Budgeting Efforts

While it's important to reward yourself for financial milestones, non-financial rewards can also be effective in reinforcing budgeting efforts and maintaining motivation. Here are some non-financial rewards to consider:

1. **Relaxing Activities**
   Engage in a calming activity like a warm bath, meditation, or yoga session to unwind and de-stress.

2. **Social Gatherings**
   Spend quality time with friends or family, such as hosting a potluck dinner or enjoying a picnic in the park.

3. **Personal**   **Development**

   Dedicate time to learning a new skill or hobby, like reading a book, learning a new language, or taking up a creative hobby.

4. **Outdoor**   **Activities**

   Take a walk in nature, go for a hike, or visit a local museum to refresh your mind and body.

5. **Entertainment**

   Enjoy a movie night at home with your favorite film or series, or listen to a new podcast.

➤ Incorporating these non-financial rewards into your routine can help maintain motivation and reinforce positive financial behaviors.
➤ By celebrating small financial victories and incorporating non-financial rewards, you can maintain motivation and continue making progress toward your financial goals.

Making Budgeting Part of Your Routine

Regular financial check-ins are essential for maintaining control over your finances and ensuring you stay aligned with your financial goals. By conducting weekly and monthly reviews, you can prevent financial drift, make informed decisions, and adapt to any changes in your financial situation.

Weekly Financial Review Checklist

1. **Track Your Spending:**
    a. Review all expenses from the past week.
    b. Categorize them into essential (e.g., groceries, utilities) and discretionary (e.g., dining out, entertainment) expenses.
    c. Compare actual spending to your budgeted amounts to identify any discrepancies.
2. **Assess Cash Flow:**
    a. Ensure that your income for the week covers your expenses.
    b. Identify any shortfalls and plan adjustments for the upcoming week.
3. **Review Financial Goals Progress:**
    a. Check the status of short-term savings goals (e.g., emergency fund, vacation fund).
    b. Evaluate debt repayment progress and adjust strategies if necessary.
4. **Monitor Subscriptions and Recurring Payments:**
    a. Identify any automatic payments or subscriptions.
    b. Assess their needs and cancel any that are no longer needed.
5. **Prepare for Upcoming Expenses:**
    a. Anticipate any known expenses in the coming week (e.g., bills, events).
    b. Ensure funds are allocated to cover these costs.

Monthly Financial Review Checklist

1. **Evaluate Overall Financial Health:**
   - ☐ Calculate your net worth by subtracting total liabilities from total assets.
   - ☐ Assess changes from the previous month to gauge financial progress.
2. **Review Budget Performance:**
   - ☐ Analyze monthly spending against your budget.
   - ☐ Identify areas where you stayed on track and areas needing improvement.
3. **Assess Debt Management:**
   - ☐ Review outstanding debts and interest rates.
   - ☐ Consider strategies like the debt snowball or avalanche methods to accelerate repayment.
4. **Evaluate Savings and Investments:**
   - ☐ Check contributions to savings accounts, retirement funds, and other investments.
   - ☐ Ensure you're on track to meet your financial goals.
5. **Review Financial Goals:**
   - ☐ Assess progress toward both short-term and long-term financial goals.
   - ☐ Adjust goals or strategies as needed based on current financial status.
6. **Plan for Future Expenses:**
   - ☐ Anticipate significant expenses in the coming months (e.g., holidays, vacations).
   - ☐ Adjust your budget and savings plan to accommodate these costs.

The Importance of Regular Financial Check-Ins

Regular financial reviews help you stay connected with your financial situation, allowing you to make informed decisions and adjust your plans as needed. This proactive approach prevents financial drift, where small, unnoticed changes can lead to significant financial challenges over time. By consistently monitoring your finances, you can maintain control, stay motivated, and work effectively toward your financial goals.

Incorporating these weekly and monthly check-ins into your routine fosters financial discipline and empowers you to make adjustments that align with your evolving financial objectives.

Avoiding Budget Burnout

Managing your finances effectively is a journey that requires balance and self-care. To prevent burnout and maintain motivation, it's essential to take regular breaks, adjust your goals as needed, and engage with supportive financial communities.

Avoiding Financial Burnout

1. **Take Regular Breaks:**
    a. Engage in activities that relax and rejuvenate you, such as walking, reading, or practicing mindfulness.
    b. Incorporate short breaks into your daily routine to reduce stress and maintain focus. MHCS San Diego
2. **Adjust Your Goals:**
    a. Regularly review your financial objectives to ensure they remain realistic and aligned with your current circumstances.
    b. Be flexible and willing to modify your goals to prevent feelings of overwhelm. Medical News Today
3. **Join Supportive Financial Communities:**
    a. Connect with others who share similar financial goals and challenges.
    b. Participate in online forums, local groups, or social media communities to exchange advice and encouragement.

Recommended Financial Resources

To continue learning and stay inspired, consider exploring the following podcasts, blogs, and books:

A. **Planet Money**
An engaging podcast that explains complex economic concepts in an accessible and entertaining way. The Investor's Podcast

B. **The Dave Ramsey Show**
Offers practical advice on budgeting, debt management, and financial planning. EmPeople

C. **The Psychology of Money by Morgan Housel**
Explores the emotional and psychological aspects of financial decisions. The Wall Street Journal

D. **Your Money or Your Life by Vicki Robin and Joe Dominguez**
Provides a comprehensive program for transforming your relationship with money. The Wall Street Journal

E. **BiggerPockets Money Podcast**
   Focuses on personal finance strategies, including investing and financial independence. The Investor's Podcast

By integrating these practices and resources into your routine, you can maintain a healthy balance between financial diligence and personal well-being, ensuring sustained progress toward your financial goals.

Chapter 8: Thriving with Your New Budget

Enjoying the Benefits of Financial Confidence

Visualizing a future free from financial stress can be a powerful motivator on your journey toward financial freedom. By imagining a life where financial concerns no longer dominate your thoughts, you can create a clear and compelling vision that guides your actions.

Success Stories of Individuals Achieving Financial Freedom

Learning from those who have successfully navigated the path to financial independence can provide valuable insights and inspiration. Here are some notable examples:

A. **Warren Buffett**: Master of Value Investing
Starting with humble beginnings, Warren Buffett's disciplined approach to value investing transformed him into one of the world's wealthiest individuals. His story exemplifies the power of patience and strategic decision-making in building wealth.Medium

B. **Elon Musk:** Visionary Entrepreneur
Elon Musk's journey from co-founding Zip2 to leading companies like Tesla and SpaceX showcases how innovation and risk-taking can lead to substantial financial success. His story highlights the importance of pursuing visionary goals and embracing challenges. Medium

C. **Sarah's Journey:** From Debt to Financial Independence
After facing significant student loans and credit card debt, Sarah, a software engineer, adopted the principles of the FIRE (Financial Independence, Retire Early) movement. Through disciplined saving and investing, she achieved financial independence, demonstrating that with determination, anyone can overcome financial challenges. Tom Bible Law

D. **Katie and Alan:** Retiring Early Through Strategic Investing
Katie and Alan achieved early retirement by building a £2 million investment portfolio. Their story illustrates how strategic investing and frugality can lead to financial freedom, allowing them to travel the world and live on their own terms. The Scottish Sun

E. **Brionuh Jadya:** Earning Through Digital Products
At 23, Brionuh Jadya transitioned from a traditional 9-to-5 job to earning $1,000 to $5,000 weekly by creating and selling digital products. Her success underscores the potential of leveraging skills and technology to achieve financial independence. The Sun

These stories demonstrate that with determination, strategic planning, and a clear vision, achieving financial freedom is within reach. By visualizing your desired future and learning from those who have succeeded, you can create a roadmap to financial security and peace of mind.

Setting New Goals for Continued Growth

Achieving foundational financial goals—such as building an emergency fund, eliminating high-interest debt, and establishing a retirement savings plan—lays the groundwork for pursuing more advanced objectives like purchasing a home, starting a business, or scaling investments. Once these foundational goals are met, you can focus on strategies to grow your savings and investments to achieve these advanced milestones.

1. Buying a Home

Purchasing a home is a significant financial milestone that requires careful planning and preparation.

- **Assess Your Financial Health:** Ensure you have a stable income, a good credit score, and manageable debt levels.
- **Save for a Down Payment:** Aim for at least 20% of the home's purchase price to avoid private mortgage insurance (PMI).
- **Understand Additional Costs:** Factor in property taxes, maintenance, and insurance when budgeting.
- **Explore Financing Options:** Research various mortgage products to find the best fit for your financial situation.

2. Starting a Business

Launching a business requires a combination of financial resources, strategic planning, and risk management.

- **Develop a Business Plan:** Outline your business model, target market, and financial projections.
- **Secure Funding:** Consider options like personal savings, loans, or investors to finance your startup.
- **Manage Cash Flow:** Implement effective cash flow management practices to ensure business sustainability.
- **Invest in Marketing:** Allocate funds to promote your business and attract customers.

3. Scaling Investments

Expanding your investment portfolio can accelerate wealth accumulation.

- **Diversify Your Portfolio:** Invest across various asset classes—stocks, bonds, real estate—to spread risk.
- **Increase Investment Contributions:** Gradually raise the amount you invest to build wealth over time.

- **Consider Real Estate:** Investing in rental properties can provide passive income and potential appreciation.
- **Explore Alternative Investments:** Investigate options like peer-to-peer lending or venture capital for higher returns.

Growing Savings and Investments Post-Foundational Goals

After securing your foundational financial goals, focus on strategies to enhance your savings and investments:

- **Automate Savings:** Set up automatic transfers to savings and investment accounts to ensure consistent contributions.
- **Maximize Retirement Contributions:** Contribute the maximum allowable amount to retirement accounts like 401(k)s or IRAs to benefit from tax advantages.
- **Reinvest Earnings:** Reinvest dividends and interest to take advantage of compound growth.
- **Regularly Review and Adjust Portfolio:** Assess your investment portfolio periodically to ensure it aligns with your financial goals and risk tolerance.

By systematically approaching these advanced financial goals and implementing strategies to grow your savings and investments, you can build a secure and prosperous financial future.

Inspiring Others to Budget

Sharing your budgeting knowledge and success stories can have a profound impact on your community, fostering a culture of financial literacy and empowerment. By openly discussing your experiences and strategies, you not only reinforce your own financial habits but also inspire and educate others to take control of their financial futures.

Benefits of Sharing Financial Knowledge

- **Empowerment Through Education:** Sharing your budgeting experiences can empower others to make informed financial decisions, leading to improved financial well-being. El Sol Nec
- **Community Economic Growth:** When individuals within a community are financially literate, they are more likely to start businesses, invest locally, and contribute to economic stability. Medium
- **Strengthening Social Bonds:** Discussing financial strategies and successes can build trust and solidarity, creating a supportive network where individuals help each other achieve financial goals.

Practical Ways to Share Your Knowledge

- **Host Workshops or Seminars:** Organize local events to teach basic budgeting, share personal success stories, and provide practical tips.
- **Start a Financial Literacy Blog or Podcast:** Create a platform to discuss budgeting strategies, interview financial experts, and share resources.
- **Volunteer for Financial Education Programs:** Partner with organizations that offer financial literacy courses to mentor and guide others.
- **Engage on Social Media:** Use platforms like Facebook, Instagram, or LinkedIn to share budgeting tips, success stories, and resources with a broader audience.

Inspiring Examples of Knowledge Sharing

- **Financial Literacy in the Military:** The UK's Royal Marines have introduced financial literacy training to enhance the financial decision-making of their personnel, aiming to improve their financial well-being and stability. Financial Times
- **Community Empowerment Through Financial Education:** Initiatives that focus on increasing financial literacy have led to more productive, economically independent communities, highlighting the importance of sharing financial knowledge. ResearchGate

By sharing your budgeting knowledge and success stories, you contribute to a ripple effect of financial empowerment, helping individuals and communities achieve greater financial stability and success.

Conclusion

Recap of the 8 Steps

Achieving financial freedom involves a structured approach. Here's a summary of the key steps:

1. **Define Your Financial Freedom**: Clearly articulate what financial freedom means to you, setting specific and measurable goals.
2. **Create a Budget**: Develop a detailed budget to track income and expenses, ensuring you live within your means.
3. **Establish an Emergency Fund**: Save at least three to six months' worth of living expenses to protect against unexpected financial setbacks.
4. **Eliminate High-Interest Debt**: Prioritize paying off debts with high interest rates to reduce financial strain.
5. **Save and Invest**: Regularly contribute to savings and investment accounts to build wealth over time.
6. **Plan for Retirement**: Contribute to retirement accounts like 401(k)s or IRAs to secure your financial future.
7. **Protect Your Assets**: Obtain necessary insurance to safeguard against potential risks.
8. **Review and Adjust Regularly**: Consistently monitor your financial plan and make adjustments as needed to stay on track.

Your Financial Freedom Plan

To solidify your action plan, consider utilizing financial planning worksheets. These tools can help you set clear goals, track progress, and stay motivated. Here are some recommended resources:

A. **My New Money Goal Worksheet**
   This worksheet assists in setting specific financial goals, determining the amount to save, and establishing a timeline.
   Consumer Finance Files

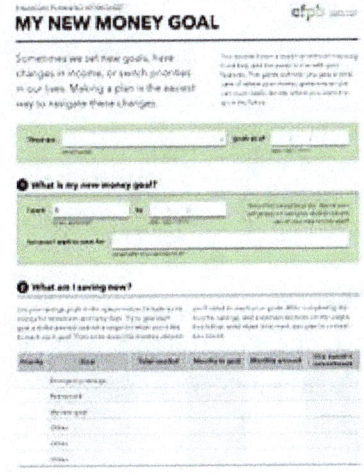

B. **Financial Freedom Worksheets**

A comprehensive set of worksheets designed to help you plan and track your journey toward financial freedom. Squarespace

C. **My Financial Freedom Worksheet**

This worksheet helps create awareness of your finances and assists in planning for your financial dreams and goals. Positively Jane

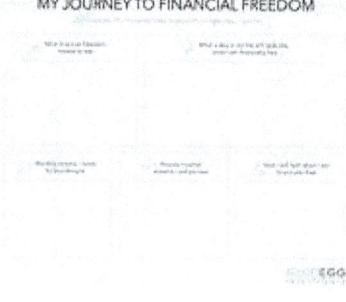

D. **Financial Planning Worksheets**

A collection of worksheets to help you set up a budget, establish goals, track spending, and determine your net worth. WPCU

E. **Financial Freedom Plan Worksheet**
   This worksheet guides you through creating a plan to achieve financial freedom, including setting goals and tracking progress.
   The Financial Diet

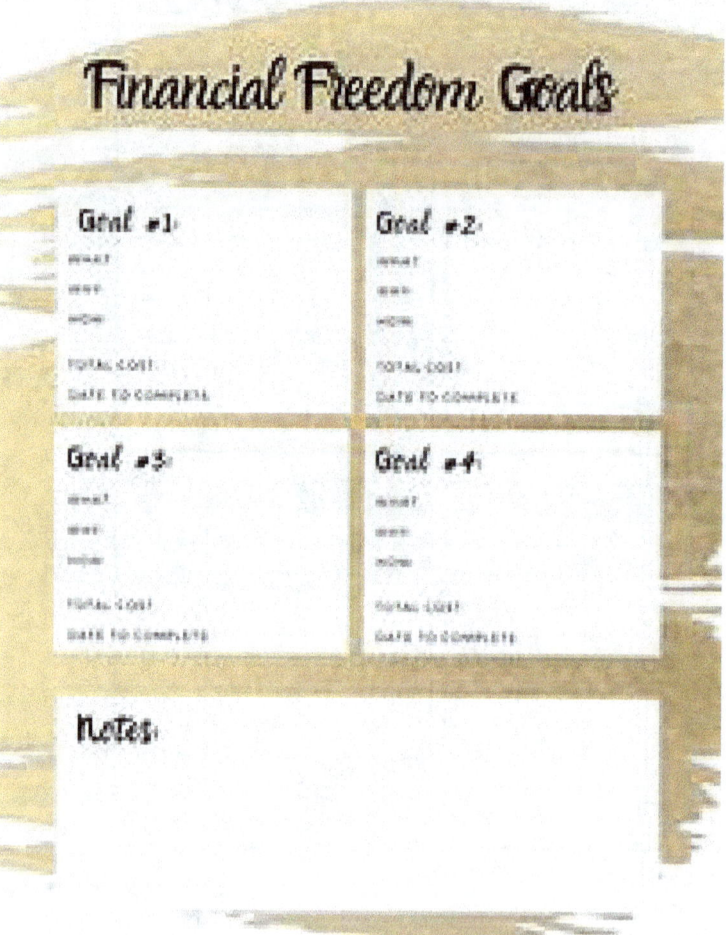

> By completing these worksheets, you can create a personalized financial plan that aligns with your goals and circumstances.

Final Motivation

Remember, the journey to financial freedom is a marathon, not a sprint. With dedication, discipline, and the right tools, you have the power to take control of your financial future and achieve your dreams. Stay focused, stay informed, and keep moving forward—your financial freedom awaits.

Appendices and Resources

Creating a personalized budget is essential for achieving financial stability and reaching your financial goals. Below are resources to assist you in this process:

Sample Budget Templates for Different Income Levels

Tailoring your budget to your income level ensures it accurately reflects your financial situation. Here are some resources offering customizable budget templates:

Microsoft Excel Budget Template
Offers a variety of pre-made templates for different budgeting needs, including household and event budgets. NerdWallet

Google Sheets Budget Template
Provides templates for monthly and annual budgets, accessible and editable online. NerdWallet

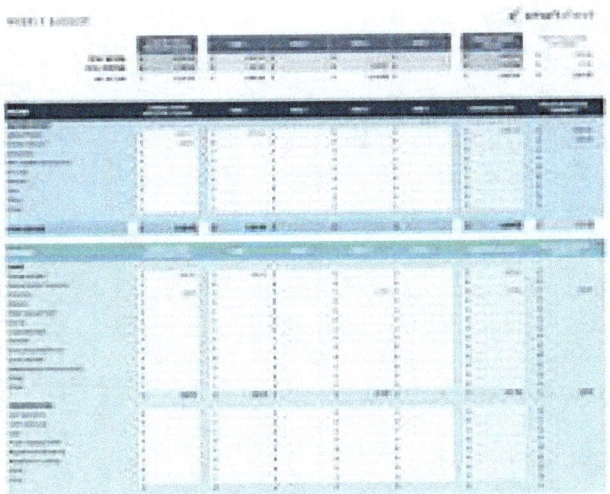

NerdWallet's Budget Planner
Allows input of monthly income and expenses to compare your finances with the 50/30/20 budget breakdown. NerdWallet

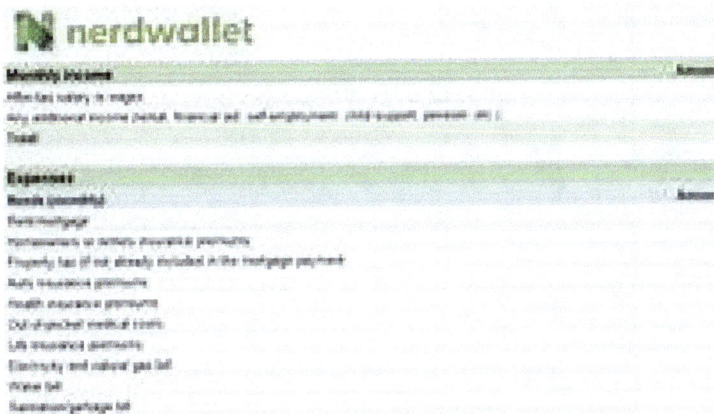

Smartsheet Budget Templates

Offers a selection of free budget templates for personal and business use. Smartsheet

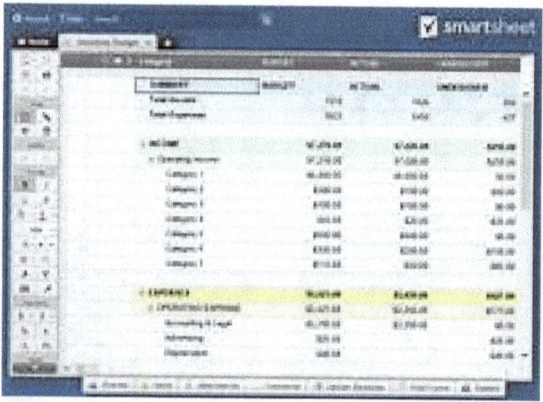

Ramsey Solutions Budget Template

Provides a free, easy-to-use budget template to help you manage your finances. Ramsey Solutions

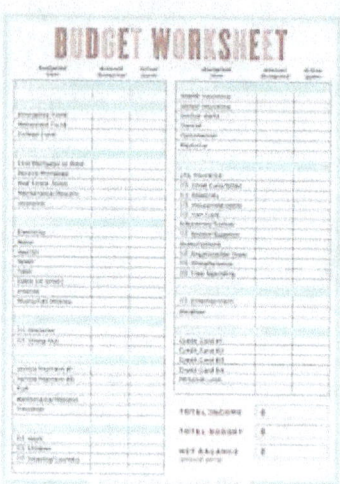

Financial Goal-Setting Worksheets

Setting clear financial goals is crucial for effective budgeting. Here are some worksheets to assist you:

- **Make a Budget Worksheet**: Helps you track your spending and plan for the next month's budget. Consumer.gov
- **Financial Planning Worksheets**: A collection of worksheets to help you set up a budget, establish goals, track spending, and determine your net worth. SMMC

Recommended Budgeting Apps and Tools

Utilizing budgeting apps can streamline the budgeting process and provide real-time insights into your finances. Here are some recommended apps:

You Need a Budget (YNAB)

Ideal for individuals aiming to pay off debt or reach savings goals, offering tools like budget creation, goal tracking, and reports. I Will Teach You To Be Rich

Mint

A free budgeting app that tracks your spending, categorizes expenses, and provides insights into your financial habits. U.S. News Money

EveryDollar

A budgeting app that helps you plan and track your spending, with a focus on zero-based budgeting. U.S. News Money

Goodbudget

A virtual envelope budgeting app that allows you to plan and track your spending across multiple devices. U.S. News Money

PocketGuard

An app that helps you track your spending and find opportunities to save by analyzing your income and expenses. U.S. News Money

Further Reading and Resources for Continued Financial Education

Expanding your financial knowledge can enhance your budgeting skills and overall financial literacy. Here are some recommended resources:

- **"Mastering Financial Goal Setting" by WellCents**: An article discussing different systems and tools for financial goal setting. MyWellCents
- **"The 35 Top Budgeting Apps and Personal Finance Tools You Need" by Purdue Global**: A guide to the best personal finance apps, tools, websites, and books to help you stick to a budget and grow your savings. Purdue Global

By utilizing these templates, worksheets, apps, and resources, you can create a budget that aligns with your financial goals and continue to enhance your financial literacy.

www.ingramcontent.com/pod-product-compliance
Lightning Source LLC
Chambersburg PA
CBHW070150230526
45471CB00002B/595